Pastels for Beginners

Pastels for Beginners
Ernest Savage

Studio Vista   London

Watson-Guptill Publications   New York

General editor Jean Richardson
© Ernest Savage 1966
Published in London by Studio Vista Limited
Blue Star House, Highgate Hill, London N19
and in New York by Watson-Guptill Publications
165 West 46th Street, New York
Reprinted 1967
Library of Congress Catalog Card Number 66-13005
Set in Folio Grotesque 8 and 9 pt.
Printed in the Netherlands
by N.V. Grafische Industrie Haarlem

SBN: Hardcover 289. 36994.0
     Paperback 289. 36926.6

Contents

Foreword

by Jack Merriott
V.P.R.I., R.O.I., S.M.A., P.S.

I am very happy to have the privilege of writing a foreword to this book on pastels by my good friend Ernest Savage, a brother member of the Pastel Society in London. The pastel is a very beautiful medium, and any book which will encourage its greater use and exploitation is performing a valuable service in introducing to the novice a fresh and delightful means of self-expression. Mr. Savage, besides being an accomplished exponent, is quite a remarkable teacher; this will be heartily endorsed by all those who have the pleasure of knowing him, and I am sure that all readers of his book will benefit greatly from the knowledge and experience he is passing on for their fuller enjoyment of life.

Polperro, January 1965.

1 Introduction

The charm of pastel

There is something very attractive and unique about the pastel medium, which may explain the increased use being made of it today by professional and amateur artists alike. Contrary to popular belief, pastel is very reliable and durable, and not at all fragile or short lived. Providing it has the same care bestowed upon it that we normally give to works of art, the pastel picture is completely permanent. Its colours do not fade or darken, and as can be seen in the pictures by the old masters, the freshness and bloom of a pastel remains as fresh as the moment it was applied.

Its use and adaptability

Amateurs could not wish for a more adaptable and exciting medium. Pastel is capable of a wide range of uses, from the tentative sketch, the quick note to capture a fleeting atmospheric effect, to a well considered and completed picture. Most painters are constant in their desire to achieve a broad and loose style in their work, whatever medium they work in, for this is the trend in present day visual expression. Weekend painters using oils or watercolours strive for this modern look, and envy the verve and lively movement displayed in the works of their more capable contemporaries. If you are keen to improve your technique, then a change for a while to the freedom of the soft pastel is likely to be very beneficial. Broadness of treatment is more easily attained with pastel, for almost no colour mixing is necessary. This has been done for you, by the pastel manufacturer. In a sense, when you buy your pastels, you are getting 'instant colour'. With this, you should not fail to become 'direct' in your work. Thus the purpose of this little book is to introduce painting with pastel to beginners, and to those keen amateurs who feel they are temporarily up against it with their usual medium.

You will be taken through a progression of exercises which, if enthusiastically undertaken, should help a beginner to grasp the essentials of this new medium, and the more experienced painter to gain a fuller understanding of tone and a looser method of treatment in his normal work.

About chalk and pastel

Pastels are made with chalk and pigment compressed together. An ingredient to improve the binding of the mixture is added by some makers. This increases the degree of hardness and reduces breakages, but artists need soft pastels for expressive work, and to obtain the real beauty of the medium.

Pastels cannot be too soft. Test those of various makers before you buy. As you can't have it both ways, don't be put out if your pastels continually break.

Soft pastels normally come in round, paper-covered sticks. Hard pastels are generally square in section, and are good for fine and detailed work. Most of the illustrations in this book were done with soft pastels. Conté crayon was used for the study on this page. It was fascinating to consider the origin of chalk as it was being dug at the Black Rabbit Chalk Pit, Arundel.

How you will improve

Try and work through this book with a lively interest, accepting your failures cheerfully and regarding your successes as stepping stones to further improvement. Your own attitude to drawing and painting will do much to secure this progress in your work, which can only be achieved by constantly making an effort. You will not achieve much worthwhile without real endeavour, so please don't expect it all to come easily. Above all, sketch as often as you can. Wherever you are during the course of your working day, be constantly looking at the every day scene, speculating in your mind how you can turn it into a picture. You must get into the habit of thinking things out. Fill all the odd moments you can spare actually sketching from observation. This will repay you a hundredfold, and moreover, you will find life more interesting and exciting if you try to depict the vitality and beauty of what you may have thought was commonplace.

Most of you will gain a great deal by following through the exercises and suggestions I have set for you. This experience should improve your work, when you survey the result at its best ... or at its worst? Now go and get a few materials, and begin to enjoy yourself.

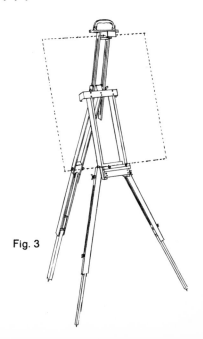

Fig. 3

2 Equipment and materials

Basic needs to start

If you are a beginner you will find it best to start with simple basic materials. All the exercises in the next chapter can be done with a few sticks of soft pastel, white and black, and a series of greys from light to dark. Get some sheets of wrapping and cartridge paper, and some sheets of tinted charcoal paper of the Ingres type. With these and a smooth board and clips, a plastic kneadable rubber, and some bits of Conté crayon and charcoal, you will be able to make a start. You will quickly begin to appreciate there is much to learn about handling pastel. Later you will need to extend your equipment for indoor and outdoor work.

Equipment for the pastellist

One thing stands out in my association with weekend and holiday painters. The progress of so many of them is curbed by unsuitable or insufficient materials. So I want to put you right from the start. Generally it is best to go for the best quality that you can afford. With some items only the best will do. This is so with an easel.

The easel It is economical to buy one that will serve for studio and outdoor work. It should therefore be portable, folding up to no more than 24 inches and weighing no more than five pounds. It should stand firmly, and take working

Fig. 4

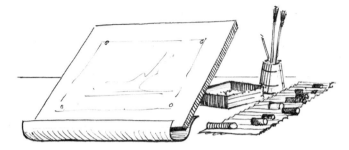

Fig. 5

pressures on the surface of the board upon it, which can be
fixed either vertically, or horizontally as a table. You should
be able to sit or stand before it. When you buy it, get the
salesman to erect it in the shop, and press on the board
fixed to it. If it whips up and slaps you in the face, or the
whole thing collapses, you will know it is useless for pastel
work. So many times my pupils bring me the easel they
have just acquired, to be shown how to put it up. The en-
suing scene is usually worthy of music hall or vaudeville,
with the easel and tutor in a free-for-all wrestle. Figs. 3 and
4 show you the kind of easel I recommend. You will be very
glad you have taken all these precautions when you begin
to use your easel.

Drawing boards These can be of hardboard, Masonite
or plywood, or one of the heavier braced boards for indoor
work. I like a Formica-covered one for studio work. Watch
the surface of your board for irregularities of any kind, for
these will 'come up' on a pastel picture if you have not taken
the precaution of inserting a sheet of smooth paper or cardboard between the board and the working surface. Of
course, if you happen to leave your loose change between

Fig. 6

your pastel paper and your board, you can expect a result like fig. 6. For pastel work, the drawing board wants to be at an angle of 50 degrees. This allows the chalk dust to fall down the paper as you work. It's a good idea to pin a trough of stiff paper along the bottom of your board, as in fig. 5, for this will catch the falling pieces. Indoors, you can use a sheet under the easel for this purpose, but this is a must for outside work, especially when your sketching location is on grass or stones. This will save you from losing the last piece of a pastel you have. My drawing of the outside gear shows the easel erected on the sheet. (See fig. 8.)

You can make a very useful portable drawing board that will also hold your papers flat and lessen the risk of rubbing your work as you carry it home. Glue a narrow fillet of wood round the back edge of the board, forming a sort of tray. Not only will this strengthen the plywood board, but with a few brass buttons on the fillet, your papers and drawings can be placed in the tray and protected by a thin sheet of cardboard, fastened in with the buttons. You can make this to suit the size of your normal work. My portable board takes a 19″ x 25″ sheet.

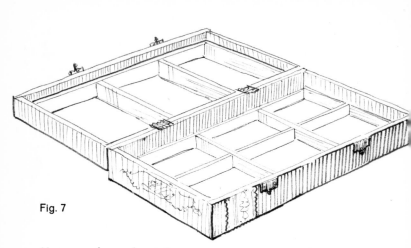

Fig. 7

Home-made equipment

The do-it-yourself types can find plenty of opportunity to make items of equipment. My favourite cases for holding pastels have been made out of large cigar boxes. With strip balsa wood, balsa cement, cardboard and pins, trays to carry pastels can be made to fit into the cigar box. A razor blade is the only tool needed. My cigar boxes are partitioned off, and have one tray that rests on the lower partitioning. When working, the tray goes into the open lid of the box. (See fig. 7.) Use plenty of cotton wool (absorbent cotton) for protecting the pastels, for they fracture easily, and get very dirty if they rub together. The colour of them is then very difficult to see and consequently hard to find.

Extra equipment for outdoor sketching

You will need to get a sketching bag that will hold your gear. This should be waterproof and have pockets. It is handy to have a bag that will suit other media too and that will take a quarter imperial (16″ x 12″) or half imperial (16″ x 23″) drawing board, for these sizes are useful for the watercolourist. Plastic bags that can be zipped are useful for the odds and ends, but especially for the protection of sheets of paper in the above sizes. You will need a light-weight stool. I find the type drawn in the sketch the most comfortable for work, for it is best to sit at a pastel drawing so that your boxes of pastels can be on the ground around you within easy reach. If you must stand, then you really need a lightweight table to take the boxes, or you will be for ever bending down in search of the pastel you need. I like to have a variety of lead pencils, carbon and chalk pencils for certain initial layouts and trial compositions, and for an inexpensive and most expressive drawing tool, the Japanese Pentel is difficult to beat. You should have a few hog hair (bristle) brushes for sweeping off pastel when errors occur and correction is required, and your sketch book is a must. I use a 10″ x 8″ sketch book of smooth, semi-transparent bank paper. You can get attractive spiral bound books of tinted pastel papers. I don't care too much for these for soft pastels, for drawings are subject to more rubbing in these than single sheets held in a portfolio.

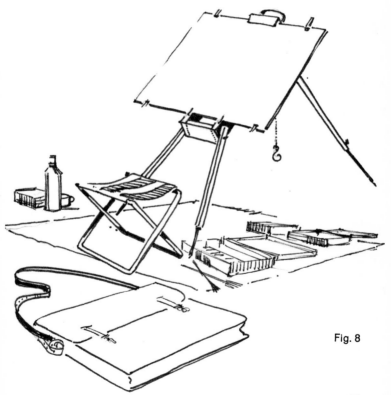

Fig. 8

Fig. 9

Layout for your studio

It is a good idea to reserve a part of your studio or work-room for the practice of pastel painting. You can then have all the necessary gear near at hand. Like an oil painter, the pastellist can set out a palette by using strips of corrugated paper, placed on the bench near the drawing board, on which he puts out the pastels in use, marking a colour reference by the side of each one. This is most useful, for it makes you become more orderly when working and will help you to save a great deal of time looking for the right pastel. When-ever I use an aerosol fixative, I do so in the bathroom, for then the air of the studio is kept free from this new, efficient, but evil smelling stuff.

Papers for the pastellist

A great deal can be written on this subject, for almost any kind of paper or cardboard can be used so long as it is not too smooth. Soft pastel requires a textured paper of interesting grain or tooth. If a tinted paper is used for an important painting, then the colour of it needs to be very permanent if the tint of the paper is made to 'work' for the artist.

Most pastellists use Ingres paper, which has a most expressive grain and is made in France, Italy, Sweden and America. The French Canson-Montgolfier, the British David Cox, the American Strathmore and the Swedish Tumba are all very suitable papers. It is best to get a sheet here and there of all the makes you can find, building up a small supply in some variety and experimenting with them. Although it is more unusual, white paper can be used, either directly with the pastel, or after having received a wash of watercolour, gouache or acrylic to the required colour and depth of tone.

Special papers have been made, some with a sanded surface, some like velvet. Be wary of these, at least at the start.

If you are taking your pastel work seriously, you must take great pains to study the differences in the papers you come across, their texture, degree of hardness, softness, and the ease with which you are able to mount them down on suitable cardboard for framing. Papers react to pastel in different ways. Watch out for those that actually stretch while you are working, and remember to readjust your clips or drawing pins (thumb tacks) to take up any slack. There is almost always a right and wrong side of the paper. It is easy to tell with those having watermarks, for the side that reads correctly is right.

Soft pastels for the artist

Having dealt with their composition on pp. 8-9, now for some advice about selection. This is not as easy as it sounds, for there are several manufacturers with world wide reputations, who each make between 300 and 600 different tints. Usually each maker boxes up assortments of colours from 12 to 250 sticks. Most sell their pastels in individual sticks, and it is best for a beginner to buy a suitable assortment and add to this collection single sticks of colour according to the way his own palette develops. However, it is important to know something of the numbering references of the various makes of pastel.

Makers' tint numbers explained

The pastellist is well served as regards quality and great variety, but the beginner can be confused by the exotic and unusual colour names some makers use, and by the lack of a standard system for identifying a range for colour strength. Unless you are well informed, you are unlikely to make much sense out of Sprinck's Citron No. 3 or Sunproof Yellow 11, tint 8.3, especially when the latter turns out to be green (since this yellow is mixed with a proportion of black).

Putting it as simply as possible, most makers (American, British, French) produce each individual colour in varying strengths by adding a percentage of white to give the paler tints of the original colour. For example, Rowneys of Britain make an ultramarine pastel in a range of nine tints from 0 to 8. No. 0 is the palest and No. 8 the deepest. You will find the colour name and the tint number on the label of each pastel. With some American makers, the numbering is the other way round, i.e., the lower the number the deeper the colour. These are also generally in a range of fewer tints. The Dutch firm of Talens has a different scheme altogether. Every original colour has an individual shade reference number in their Rembrandt range of pastels. Thus ultramarine deep has shade number 60. The figure five after the decimal point, viz. 60.5, means the pure tint of this blue. When the decimal changes to .6, .7, .8, .9, this indicates mixtures of the pure tint with 20%, 40%, 60% or 80% of white. Therefore 60.9 is the palest of pale blues. The great

Fig. 10

difference in the Dutch system is their mixtures of pure tint with black, and .4, .3, .2 indicate 20%, 40%, 60% of black added to the pure tint; so you can see why pastel 60.2 is so dark a blue as to be almost black. This now explains why Sunproof Yellow 11, tint 8.3, is actually green in colour, for the pure yellow has been mixed with 40% black.

This all sounds very involved. Don't let it worry you. This Dutch scheme has its advantages, especially when an artist wants to be as tonally correct as possible. But to take full advantage of the scheme, it would appear to me to be necessary to possess a maker's range of tints in chart form, and so buy pastels especially for the job on hand. These charts can be obtained from Talens, the makers of Rembrandt pastels. They are very expensive and beautifully produced, for each is coloured by hand. My own from this manufacturer is over four feet long and exhibits 500-600 hand-tinted pastel colours, each covered with an acetate window.

A beginner's assortment

You will need an assortment of about 72 tints to make a good start, and to help you with selection a chart of this number of tints is shown in colour facing p. 40. This assortment was selected by the artist Jack Merriott, and it forms a very useful basic collection of colours for all subjects. You will, of course, add to your collection as need demands.

You can use this chart for colour matching when purchasing any make of soft artists' pastel. All the well-known makes of pastel are good. For my own work I use mainly those of Rowney, who box up this 72 assortment, and also the Rembrandt pastels by Talens. In the United States, Grumbacher and Weber produce fine pastels of comparable quality which are available in assortments of various sizes and can be matched up to the tints shown in the colour chart.

To help you, the colours used in the 'How to do it' demonstrations in this book will be referred to as numbers 1 to 72 in the colour chart. In addition to the 72 assortment, you will find it very helpful to buy a full series of one of the greys, from light to dark. Cool grey in about six tones would be ideal.

Now all the gear has been dealt with, at last we can really get busy with our pastelling!

3 Making a start

It is exciting to start something new, and having got together the suggested basic materials, you will be itching to get on with it. First be sure to place a sheet of smooth paper or cardboard over your drawing board. Now clip on a sheet of ordinary brown wrapping paper, rough side up, and with a piece of white soft pastel held between thumb and index finger, begin to make strokes on the paper to get the feel of it.

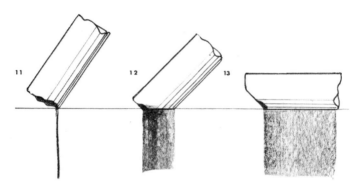

Preliminary stroke practice

Notice that by having the one inch of pastel flat on the paper, one inch bands of tint are made with each stroke. By lifting the pastel on end and edge, lines of different thicknesses are made, as in figs. 11, 12, 13. Wriggle and twist your pastel about between the finger and thumb, thus finding the sharper edges at the end of the broken pastel, and make thin and thick strokes in variation. This will give vitality to your drawing and make it lively and more expressive. Try out the same exercises with black soft pastel, using it on edge and flat to the surface. Examine the examples on this page. All are done in one stroke, and in 15, 16, 17, without the pastel being lifted from the paper. The arrows show the direction in which the pastel travelled.

Now you must begin to examine these doodling experiments and begin to learn by thinking about them. This is how all artists discover or adapt themselves to new techniques. You see, as children, we begin our pictorial expressions with line drawing, mostly using a point. If you are to be successful with pastel, you must be able to do more than this and, as in the diagrams, begin to use wide lines in your work. Then you will be drawing or painting as an area or mass, which in turn is governed by a twist of the hand or flow of the arm as you try to express a form.

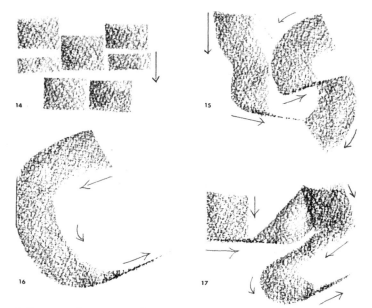

Influence of paper surfaces

Try out your soft pastel on some textured paper of the Ingres type. See how the grain of the paper influences the pastel marks made upon it. You will find also, that by increasing the pressure upon the pastel, a deeper tone is obtained. This is because the pastel has been pressed into the recesses of the grain, whereas lighter strokes pass over these indentations. In figs. 18 to 21, you will see the kind of effect the grain or tooth, as it is sometimes called, has upon the pastel strokes.

Fig. 18

18 On cheap cartridge (drawing) paper, the grain is quickly filled.

Fig. 19

19 On Ingres charcoal paper, the accent of the grain becoming more apparent.

Fig. 20

20 On canvas grained paper.

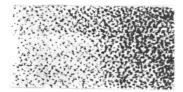

Fig. 21

21 On heavy watercolour paper where the tooth is pronounced and difficult to fill, even with heavy pressure and with two or three applications of pastel over the same spot.

Beginners will soon discover that Ingres paper, or one of similar texture, is the easiest to use and affords the most expressive surface.

Correcting errors, lifting pastel

I hope you will spend a good deal of time at this stroke practice. You will not learn much in five minutes, but if you work thoughtfully for several hours on these loosening up exercises, the experience you will gain will be worth the effort. Don't be nervous . . . be bold! Let yourself go with it.

There is no need to be worried about errors in this medium. Soft pastel is easily lifted, and this is where the hog hair (bristle) brush comes in. You simply sweep off the area to be removed, blowing away the dust as you do so. This will leave a slight stain upon the paper, and if you want to, you can get back the original surface by pressing a moulded piece of well kneaded putty rubber on to the area. Repeated pressings and rubbings with the kneadable rubber, and hey presto - you are ready to go over that part of your work again.

This is a most important technique for the beginner, and you should become adept at it by sweeping off some of your earlier experiments. In this way you will approach the correction of a more important pastel painting with greater confidence.

Paper will only take pastel up to the limit of filling the grain of it. Once the grain is filled, it is quite impossible to get any more pastel on top. If you attempt it, the pastel will skate about and leave unpleasant smeary marks in the over-loaded areas. This is a sure sign in a pastel painting that the painter is a beginner, or does not understand his materials. You can avoid these marks by (a) tentative strokes or, (b) if you have been direct and filled the grain with the wrong colour or tone of pastel, by removing it by sweeping off before repainting with the correct tint. You will find to start with, and especially when working in colour, that you will need to do this quite frequently.

Fig. 22

23

24

25

26

Imaginative compositions with one pastel

During the first stage of stroke practice, your enthusiastic appetite to advance will need feeding with more interesting subject material than lines and squiggles. When you feel the need, try inventing some little pictures of your own. Don't worry over failures. There will bound to be one or two you will like. Work in rectangles about 6″ x 8″ either way up. Use about an inch of pastel, white or black, and begin by making an impromptu squiggle almost to fill the rectangle, using the pastel flat to the surface, just like the one I did without any thought in fig. 23. Now consider the motif you have drawn, and ponder how you can turn it into a landscape with a few more well premeditated thoughts. In figs. 24, 25, and 26, I have deliberately copied the same motif as in No. 23 to show you how I have contrived to find three interesting pictures, all from the original squiggle.

The value of this sort of creative work is immense, for quite apart from helping your grasp of pictorial composition, you will learn that you can make a monochromatic picture with only one pastel simply by varying the pressure on it to

27

28

obtain different degrees of tone from light to dark. You should try this out using white on tinted paper and black pastel on white paper. (See also figs. 29 and 30.)

Direct drawings in monochrome

Although it will assist your understanding of pastel technique to doodle, to make abstractions and draw from memory, there is nothing to beat continual sketching direct from nature, that is to say, drawing from observation. Your sketch book should be with you as often as your wrist watch, and every opportunity should be taken to make sketches in pencil, ball point pen etc. Make no mistake about it, the better a draughtsman you can become, the better your pictures will be in any medium and by any method.

Study my sketches of trees (figs. 27 and 28). These were done from observation. The three pine trees are in my studio garden, and have been drawn hundreds of times by visiting pupils. Notice how I have used black chalk to obtain the true character of the trees and to portray the texture and play of light on the foliage. Copy these examples on a much larger scale, then start making similar studies of your own, to include trees, buildings, people, and so on.

Fig. 29

Making the paper 'work' for you

You will have realised for yourself how a tinted paper helps you. Later I will explain how to select tinted paper for certain subjects. But right now you must begin to learn how to get your paper to do some of the work. Since more pastel pictures are painted on toned paper than on white, it is the *light* in the picture that has to be expressed by the artist.

To explain this, I have painted two similar sketches of a village scene in Yugoslavia. I made the original sketch with a Flomaster one scorching day whilst waiting for an ancient coach to take me back to the hotel. The villagers of Moscenice gossiped beneath the shade of a huge tree. The first sketch (fig. 29) was drawn with ivory black pastel on

Fig. 30

white Ingres paper. The sun shines where the paper has been left untouched. With differing pressures on the black pastel, a variety of greys to jet black have been produced, since where the white paper peeps through the black pastel, a grey is formed. And if you don't believe it, look again at this picture through your lashes, with eyes partly closed. Now you can easily pick out the greys from the black.

In the second example (fig. 30), the process is reversed, and white pastel has been used on black paper. Once again the greys emerge, for these are the tones between white and black. In a sense, the shadows have been drawn in the first and the light in the second picture. Try out a picture of your own like fig. 30, for when you understand how the tone of the paper can help, you are on the way to success.

Many teachers use white chalk on blackboards. This is all right for notes and so on, but when it comes to drawing, how many teachers use the white chalk as light? I have frequently seen shadows represented with white chalk. This is really confusing to young and inexperienced minds, for they are being required to see and learn as from a negative. So when you use tinted paper, remember that any pastel lighter in tint than the paper is really a form of light. I have painted the light only, as the sun shines on the shepherd and his sheep, in fig. 31.

Fig. 31

Direct drawing for abstract

I am not in favour of any accidental effect in picture making. Paint thrown about on a canvas, then rolled upon, or perhaps slept upon, seems to me to require no artistic gift. Doubtless out of queer accidental forms the virile imagination of the master can develop exciting visual expression, if his mind, talent, and experience are brought to bear upon its execution. This is not for a beginner. Rather would I see you fill a rectangle as in fig. 32. In this, the mind has been active and the pastel used in broad, expressive sweeps to create a satisfying pattern. Try your hand at building up an abstract composition, for again, whether you like the result or not, you will still be practicing the use of pastel, and you will gain from the experience.

Fig. 32

Pastel painting in tones

This word *tone* is constantly cropping up. If you move among painters you will hear it often. It is important, and you must understand it. Although some treat it so, there is no mystery about tone. But it is made rather difficult for the beginner when he hears such words or phrases as 'the tonal value', 'a low key', 'that needs to be lowered', 'you need a wider scale', 'your tones don't read', and so on. Well, don't worry, they all refer to tone. You must not only be able to understand the principles of tone, but you must also be able to *see* and *portray* tone.

Simply put, tone is the relationship between white and black or, if you like, light and dark. It is most easily seen in degrees of greys. In the tone chart (fig. 33), a medium grey paper was chosen as halfway between white and black, and then a scale of five tones was created with white and black pastel and the tint of the paper; the tone lowers from white to black; the tone gets higher from black to white. Tone is more difficult to see when associated with colour, and we shall have a special lesson on this later on. Tone is important, for it helps to describe the form or shape of an object, and with tone the artist expresses distance, or recession, as it is sometimes called.

The tonal sketch (fig. 34) of Polperro harbour, in Cornwall, depicts the use of the scale of tones shown in fig. 33. The dark behind the old pilchard boat is almost black, and the highest tone is seen on the angled edge of the right-hand cottage and on the dinghy tied up to the large boat. Now treat this as an exercise.

Fig. 33

Step-by-step hints to painting Polperro harbour

On medium grey paper draw a vertical rectangle 7" x 12", or even larger, but to this scale.

1 With charcoal draw an outline of the composition.

2 Boldly place the highest light and then the darkest dark, with some pressure on the white or black pastel. Now examine the effect.

3 With lighter strokes, using the pastel flat to the surface, register the half tones, remembering to leave some areas of paper free from any pastel.

4 Complete the picture with fine lines made by the edge of the pastel, to capture texture of rock and timber and the reflections in the water.

Fig. 34

More studies in tone

Examine the two-tone charts on this page. Squint at them through your eyelashes. Each is a scale of six tones. Fig. 35 ranges from white to black, with the third tone down provided by the tint of the paper. Fig. 36 has been prepared in a series of cool grey pastel. The first is the widest scale possible, like the top to the bottom note on the piano. The second chart is a narrower scale, thus the changes in tone are more subtle. Nature is more like the second scale. The first is brash and strident, but much easier to discern. You should now obtain a complete series of grey pastel from the lightest to deepest tone, and practice with them. You will find them delightful to handle, and capable of far reaching experiment.

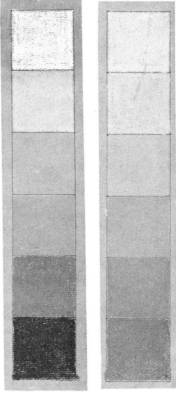

Fig. 35,   Fig. 36

A landscape in six tones

I want you now to share my excitement at painting in the Highlands of Scotland. We have arrived on the shores of Loch Duich, and behind the clump of fir trees we can see the mountain mass of the Isle of Skye. I expect the lonely fisherman hopes for a good catch, but we settle down with our equipment to express the grandeur of the mountain scene in a simple manner. You will need a scale of pastels like that in fig. 35, so take out your black and white, and three tints of cool grey.

Fig. 37 **Loch Duich**

Stage one (Fig. 37)

In a rectangle drawn to scale, say 12″ x 16″, make an outline drawing in charcoal, taking care to keep the proportion
of the mountain masses, the tree and cottage group, and the
level of the water line. I have decided that the mountains of
Skye and the ruffle of water beneath the dark hills of the
mainland shall be the paper left *untouched*. These areas
must 'work' for us, and they will add luminosity and distance
to our attempt. So keep these parts clean at all costs. If you
smudge, clean up with putty rubber. Start painting the sky-
line with white, pressing the pastel into the paper as you
work along the upper edge to form an impression of clouds.
Use less pressure at the top, until with this one pastel your
work looks like fig. 37.

Fig. 38 **Loch Duich**

Second stage (Fig. 38)

With the lightest cool grey overpaint the top of the sky, bringing it into the white already placed. With the same pastel indicate the right-hand, rising, rock-strewn ground at the roadside and the light on the cottage wall, for what sun there is, is shining from left to right. With the darkest cool grey put in the right-hand hills, pressing hard where a silhouette occurs against the light, but slackening pressure to indicate rock formation. Really press hard when you put in the reflection of these hills. Now examine your work. Notice that the mountains of Skye are already 'going back' to the eye, and there is luminosity in them because the paper has been left without pastel.

Fig. 39 **Loch Duich**

Final stage (Fig. 39)

Complete the bottom of the reflection to the shore with medium cool grey and with the same pastel indicate road shadows, rock surfaces in the immediate foreground and the side of the cottage facing us. With black pastel carefully put in the fir trees which are the centre of interest in the picture. Be careful to leave the shape of roofs and so on. Finish your picture with touches of tone about the shore, road and foreground rocks, and carefully depict the lonely fisherman in black, for he helps to balance the dark tree mass.

This exercise is worth doing several times, so make a tracing of your first drawing so you will not have this effort again.

4 Using soft pastels

Get to know your pastels

The first essential on obtaining a box of soft pastels is to become thoroughly acquainted with the tint of every pastel in the box. The quickest way to know your colours is to make a personal tint chart of all the pastels you have. This will help you in other ways, for your chart becomes a matching device when painting, and a reference when purchasing further supplies or when you are forced to accept the nearest shade to that required, or one from another maker's range.

Some makers supply a printed chart with their larger boxed assortments, ready for you to fill in the pastel colours and make a note of each colour name, tint and number. If you give your handmade chart a spray of aerosol fixative, it will last for some time.

As you get working with pastels, you will soon find that even with 72 your range is very limited and more will be required. This becomes very obvious when you think of the thousands of different tints one can make with a dozen watercolours with the various permutations of mixing and of strength according to the amount of water used. No wonder we constantly hear a limited palette of colours advised. One of the advantages of pastel painting is that it is customary to work with a smaller range of tints as compared with other media, and this encourages you to think a great deal more about your colour schemes and the effect that one colour has upon another.

If you do a lot of landscape painting, you cannot have too many greys, and many of the more neutral earthy colours like raw umber, burnt umber and light red are excellent in their lighter tints.

Facing p. 40 is a full colour chart showing all the tints in the selection of 72 pastels. This should be of great assistance to the beginner. By seeing all the tints at once, it is possible to appreciate the subtle shades of the pastels, and to notice that bright pure colours are few. The colours in this chart have been arranged approximately in spectrum order, to limit any effect one tint would have upon its neighbour.

Making a start with colour

When you begin to use your pastels, break off a piece from the end of the stick. Don't be tempted to work with the whole stick with its paper wrapper on. If you do, your work will become niggly and tight. You need ½" to 1" pieces to express a broad and free treatment. Occasionally you will come across a stick of pastel that seems to fall into a powder as soon as you start to unwrap it. This happens to about one in twenty of the very softest pastels, and the only way to make use of them is to keep the wrapper on for as long as possible.

In trying a new technique, it sometimes helps to use a subject with which you are already familiar. So let's repeat the Polperro harbour drawing (page 31) in a vertical rectangle 10½" x 18". Choose a cool grey Ingres paper, and leave space down one side of it to try out your colours before applying them. In making your picture in colour, try to benefit from the previous exercise which was in tones of grey. When choosing colours, think about tones, for these too must be correct in their degree of lightness or darkness. Do not use white or black pastel. The dark shadow behind the pilchard boat will be a cool grey similar to No. 39 in the colour chart facing p. 40. For the left-hand cottage walls use a light yellow ochre (6), and for right-hand wall light red (27). Use your pastels boldly, with broad flat strokes. When you have painted the darkest and lightest parts of the picture as indicated above, use green grey (71) and warm grey (38) for the cliff face that goes up behind the cottages to the top of the picture. Using bluish purple (45), finish the gap between the cottages where the rough hewn steps inch their way up the cliffside to the next terrace of cottages above.

Now this has got you started, and with every new pastel used you will become more familiar with them. You can now complete the picture of Polperro Harbour and enjoy yourself depicting the reflections of the blue pilchard boat. Remember to make use of the colour of your paper, which can represent parts of the grey Cornish rock and the slate roofs of the fishermen's cottages. If you are not happy with parts of your work, sweep off the pastel with a brush, touch up the spot with a putty rubber (kneaded rubber), and then repaint. This is all excellent practice.

Demonstration painting: 15th-century Sussex bridge

A five-minute drive from my studio takes us to Stopham bridge, with its tall central arch flanked on each side with three lower arches, all partitioned with stately buttresses. This beautiful seven arched bridge is one of the oldest packhorse bridges in Britain, and where the gentle Rother flows beneath it to join the river Arun is a favourite spot for anglers as well as sketchers.

This is a difficult subject for beginners to tackle, but it is one that introduces many features that need explanation, and so gives help to the amateur.

I made my first sketches for this chapter one sunny afternoon in April. The branches on the pollarded willows by the water's edge were almost orange in the direct sunlight, and the trees beyond the bridge were still without leaf. I was enthralled with the way that the shadow side of the buttresses wrinkled their lazy reflections in the slow moving water. I made a quick monochromatic sketch with four tones of neutral grey, black and white pastel. A blue grey Ingres paper was used, which had been mounted down on pasteboard 12" x 16". This sketch is reproduced in fig. 40. Next day, same time (and sun still shining), I made a full colour sketch, after making a number of alternative black and white compositions. With this material, I worked up the picture for your instruction in four stages.

Now a word about materials used in the demonstration.

The paper

There always has to be some thought about the tint of the paper to be used for a given picture, and it must be made to help the effect you are trying to create. Often a drawing can be spoilt by the wrong choice of paper. It is so easily done, when in haste. I did this a few weeks ago when trying to capture the coldness of the snow as it swirled among the trees at the foot of the South Downs. I used the first piece of paper out of the bag: it was a warm fawn. Because of this initial mistake, extra work had to be put in to 'lose' the background tint. So take care when you select your paper.

No mistake was made this time, for contemplating the sunlight on the bridge and the shadows the buttresses cast on

Fig. 40 **Stopham Bridge** Pastel in monochrome, 12″ x 16″

the stone, I chose the colour of the paper to match, as near as possible, that of the reflections of these shadows. The paper selected was a Swedish Tumba tint called Heather No. 238, a warm putty coloured grey with flecks of red and green in the characteristic Ingres grain.

The pastels

Have a strip of corrugated paper ready to receive your bits of pastel as they are named in colour and tint. Have about an inch of each, and as you get it from the box, mark the edge of the corrugation with the colour before you set it down. This will help you to find a particular piece quickly, and begins the habit of a tidy and thoughtful approach to your work. I used about 24 pastels to paint this picture.

The Jack Merriott assortment of 72 pastels by Rowney

Names from left to right.
Line 1 Cadmium Primrose 6, Cadmium Lemon 3, Cadmium Lemon 1
         Naples Yellow 6, Naples Yellow 2, Yellow Ochre 0
Line 2 Yellow Ochre 6, Yellow Ochre 2, Cadmium Red Orange 6
         Cadmium Red Orange 2, Cadmium Red Orange 1, Rose Madder 2
Line 3 Poppy Red 8, Cadmium Red 6, Cadmium Red 1
         Indian Red 5, Indian Red 3, Indian Red 1
Line 4 Madder Brown 8, Purple Lake 7, Burnt Sienna 7
         Burnt Sienna 6, Burnt Sienna 4, Burnt Sienna 0
Line 5 Light Red 4, Light Red 2, Light Red 0
         Red Grey 4, Red Grey 1, Vandyke Brown 2
Line 6 Vandyke Brown 6, Sepia 8, Sepia 3
         Raw Umber 6, Raw Umber 4, Warm Grey 1
Line 7 Warm Grey 5, Warm Grey 3, Cool Grey 5
         Cool Grey 3, Cool Grey 1, Neutral Grey 2
Line 8 Reddish Purple 5, Bluish Purple 6, Bluish Purple 3
         French Ultramarine 6, Cornflower Blue 6, Cornflower Blue 2
Line 9 Cobalt 3, Cobalt 0, Indigo 4
         Indigo 1, Blue Grey 6, Ivory Black
Line 10 Lizard Green 8, Sap Green 3, Sap Green 1
         Olive Green 4, Olive Green 0, Sprinck's Citron 1
Line 11 Viridian 6, Terre Verte 5, Hooker's Green 5
         Brilliant Emerald 3, Hooker's Green 1, Emerald Green 1
Line 12 Sprinck's Citron 3, Willow Green 5, Sprinck's Olive 3
         Green Grey 4, Green Grey 1, Brilliant White

Rembrandt soft pastels: Talens and Sons Inc. Union N.J., U.S.A.

The following assortment of pastels have been especially selected by the author to correspond
to the selection of tints reproduced opposite. Ask for a box that will hold 96 pastels in which
to put your first 72. You will find equivalent colours manufactured by other leading American
firms, like M. Grumbacher, Inc., and F. Weber Co.
Line 1 11.5 Cadmium Yellow Light, 11.7 Cadmium Yellow Light, 11.9 Cadmium Yellow Light
         12.6 Cadmium Yellow Deep, 12.9 Cadmium Yellow Deep, 20.9 Light Yellow Ochre
Line 2 20.5 Light Yellow Ochre, 20.7 Light Yellow Ochre, 18.5 Chrome Yellow Orange
         18.7 Chrome Yellow Orange, 18.9 Chrome Yellow Orange, 38.8 Permanent Red Deep
Line 3 40.5 Cadmium Red Light, 40.7 Cadmium Red Light, 40.9 Cadmium Red Light
         28.5 Caput Mortuum Light, 28.7 Caput Mortuum Light, 28.9 Caput Mortuum Light
Line 4 41.2 Carmine Red, 49.6 Purple One, 53.4 Burnt Sienna
         53.5 Burnt Sienna, 53.7 Burnt Sienna, 53.9 Burnt Sienna
Line 5 24.6 Burnt Light Ochre, 23.7 Ochre Orange, 23.9 Ochre Orange
         56.8 Cassel Earth, 55.9 Burnt Umber, 25.9 Burnt Green Earth
Line 6 53.2 Burnt Sienna, 56.2 Cassel Earth, 54.7 Raw Umber
         54.5 Raw Umber, 54.8 Raw Umber, 54.9 Raw Umber
Line 7 78.6 Mouse Grey, 78.8 Mouse Grey, 64.5 Grey Blue
         64.7 Grey Blue, 64.9 Grey Blue, 77.11 Grey
Line 8 51.5 Red Violet, 57.6 Blue Violet, 57.8 Blue Violet
         59.5 Ultramarine Light, 60.5 Ultramarine Deep, 60.9 Ultramarine Deep
Line 9 48.6 Cobalt Blue, 48.9 Cobalt Blue, 48.3 Cobalt Blue
         62.9 Green Blue, 65.4 Blue Green, 5.5 Black
Line 10 72.5 Permanent Green Light, 68.6 Chrome Green Light, 68.8 Chrome Green Light
         74.6 Grey Blue, 64.9 Grey Blue, 70.9 Deep Green
Line 11 67.5 Viridian, 67.4 Viridian, 71.5 Permanent Green Deep
         71.7 Permanent Green Deep, 71.8 Permanent Green Deep, 71.9 Permanent Green Deep
Line 12 72.3 Permanent Green Light, 74.4 Olive Green, 20.3 Light Yellow Ochre
         73.2 Moss Green, 80.7 Green Grey, 1.5 White

40

1
2
3
4
5
6
7
8
9
10
11
12
13
14
15
16
17
18
19
20
21
22
23
24
25
26
27
28
29
30
31
32
33
34
35
36
37
38
39
40
41
42
43
44
45
46
47
48
49
50
51
52
53
54
55
56
57
58
59
60
61
62
63
64
65
66
67
68
69
70
71
72

Stage one, Fig. 42

Draw on the selected paper a rectangle 12″ x 16″ and with a soft pencil rule off two inch squares to form a grid to help you accurately to enlarge the drawing in fig. 42. I was above the level of the tops of the smaller arches, so these run upwards in a line as they recede. Make sure any lines that should be vertical are really upright. You should make a habit, especially in the early stages of your work, of starting off any picture with good drawing. You are on your way to success if you do this, for when your composition is settled and drawing completed, it is something less to worry about. If you make your first drawing with charcoal, some will brush off where needed. If you use black Conté crayon which makes a more permanent line, remember to keep the upper surfaces of objects in as fine a line as possible, reserving the thicker blacker stroke for shadow sides. Don't draw the cloud formations with black lines.

It was necessary in my own drawing to make it distinct enough for you to copy, thus some of my lines are over black. It is always good practice to avoid over black lines in highlighted parts of a drawing.

Stage two, Fig. 43

It is now time to prepare a lighter ground to receive the sky painting. Start this by painting the sky with cool grey (41), adding white (72) at the horizon above the trees. Rub this in gently with a small wad of cotton wool (absorbent wool). Then use the same chalk-impregnated wad to rub in a tone on the sunlit parts of the bridge and the sky reflection at the bottom left-hand corner. Don't rub any black drawing into this. If you do, lift it with putty rubber (kneaded rubber). Now brush off the sky to remove loose pastel, taking care not to smear the parts of the paper you want left untouched. This preparation helps to lighten the dark paper, and makes the final painting of the sky easier and less laboured in appearance. Remember this is only a suggested passage of light, as you will see in the unfinished portions of the sky in the colour reproduction of stage three.

Now with yellow ochre (6), gently paint this warm tint into the sunlit parts of the clouds and more directly into the bridge, with special emphasis on light edges left and top, where the ancient sandstone catches more light. Next register the dark under the arches using cool grey (39), start-

Fig. 42

Fig. 43

Fig. 44

Fig. 45

ing from the farthest arch and running the same colour into the reflection, but with less pressure to the pastel, so that more paper shows through and lightens the tone of the reflection. Do all the arch shadows and reflections this way, but afterwards, starting from the third arch from the left, gradually introduce amounts of blue grey (53) into the arch shadows, so that the nearest arch becomes the darkest. This should give the effect of recession and atmosphere between the first and last arch, because each lightens gradually as it goes farther back. Whilst using blue grey (53), indicate broadly the shape of the fir tree mass top left.

Stage three, Fig. 44

We must now give attention to the sky and finish this part of our picture completely. In fig. 44, part of the sky has been left to show the extent of the first groundwork, which you can see was very slight but enough to lighten the paper. With cool grey (41), work on the light in the clouds, creating a cumulus effect with broad strokes that go over the pale yellow already placed. Complete the cool grey (41) to the tops of the trees, pressing rather firmly at this point. Now with pale cobalt (50), pastel into the grey under the clouds using less of it at the horizon. Pastel more areas of this light blue colour loosely above the clouds, and then with very light indigo (52) add more tone to the top of the sky. Don't put any of this darker blue beneath the clouds. In this operation we have tried to get gradation of tone into the sky by using darker tones of colour at the zenith, or top of the picture, and paler tones until the horizon is reached. Cloud shadows can now be indicated at the right side and underneath with cool grey (40). Thus we have used six different pastels to paint the sky.

The rule to remember about reflections is that generally *lights* are reflected *darker*, and *darks* are reflected *lighter*. Take every opportunity to observe real reflections and study their tones and shapes.

Now you will know why, in the previous stage, I suggested you should allow the paper to show through when pastelling the reflections of the darkened arches, for this lightens their tone. Now start painting the reflection of the sunlit stonework, using a warm grey (36) and raw umber (35). This will be less bright than their real counterpart, but be sure you get your reflections in the right place, immediately under the parts reflected.

It is a good plan to try and bring a picture along as a whole. For this reason it is unwise to spend too long concentrating on one spot. A change helps you to study the effect various colours and tones are having upon one another. So now leave the reflections for a bit and with bright yellowish green (57), boldly indicate the sunlit grass on the far bank, and with expressive smears of the same colour, the grass under the willow bushes. I expect you will notice that so far your picture seems cold, but some loose work on the right-hand branches with light red (26) will soon put this right, but let your pastel strokes follow the line of the branch growth. Now give more attention to the stonework, adding warmth to it with yellow orange (11) and with the merest touch of yellow to the nearer masonry. In this way we create colour perspective, for the farthest end of the bridge is cooler and greyer in colour, and the nearer end warmer and brighter. If you were painting a field of golden corn, you would grey off the farther side to give depth and flatness to the field.

With greyish green (68) begin to suggest the moss on the wet stone in shadow, and in the next stage try and interpret the discolouration of antiquity generally in the nearer stonework. Never emphasise detail in shadows.

Final stage, Fig. 45

You must now work on the tree groups on the left, and on their reflections. It is a good thing when faced with painting reflections to proceed with this work at the same time as you are putting in the objects reflected. You then get better placing of both, and an improved understanding of their tonal relationship. Thus with light brown (33) and warm grey (37), carefully paint the large oak tree at the end of the bridge, drawing down its reflection with light brown only. Additions to the lighter sides of the fir trees can now be made with grey green (68) and light grey green (70), using number 68 in the reflection as it is a lighter tone. Warm grey (37) will help with the shadows under the fir tree foliage down to the bushes at the foot of them. These are breaking into leaf bud and should be put in with a reddish grey (28) and a medium brown green (69), with a repeat of warm grey and bluish purple (45) for the darker areas under these waterside trees and up to the streak of sunlit grass. These last colours, grey and purple, can be used in vertical bands in the reflection. The sky in reflection should be darker than the actual sky, so use cool grey (40) with a touch of pale grey blue (52).

The picture can now be completed with final touches to the masonry, the warm reflected light under the main arch and the willows on the right with light red (25, 26, 27). Use vandyke brown (31) and warm grey (37) for the trunks and branches in shade, and the grey green (68) for the shadow side of the tallest willow tree. Don't overdo the final touches. You must stop *before* you think you are finished.

Well, I hope you enjoyed painting this grand old bridge with me. Now we must stretch our legs and go for a walk over the bridge to that little patch of sunlit grass. Come over with me in your imagination, and to help you to visualise the scene, I have drawn for you the view from the other side, which shows the ancient inn 'The White Hart' at the end from which we have been painting. A very convenient location for a morning's work, to be sure of a nice cool drink afterwards!

Now back to work. It would be excellent practice if you painted the bridge again, while you have the pastels available on the corrugated palette. This time make your drawing 15″ x 20″, marked off with 2½″ squares, for the larger the work the broader it is possible to be in your technique of handling pastels. Then, when you have completed this, have a go, on your own, at the other view showing 'The White Hart' behind the orange willows.

The White Hart, Stopham Bridge, Sussex

My drawing was done on Fabriano Ingres, pale grey. Conté crayon was used throughout, with a little white chalk for highlighted parts of the bridge. When making a picture in colour of this subject, almost the same two dozen pastels could be used as for the previous picture, with some additional ones to depict the moss-covered red clay tile of the old inn and the dark boarded lean-to on the side of the building.

This composition would look well as a large painting, and I suggest you work on a sheet of warm grey or green grey paper 18″ x 22″. Once again, use one edge of the paper to try out your colours. Try a slightly different approach by making an outline drawing with a 3B or 4B pencil. As there is very little sky in the picture, work in a very light grey

Fig. 46 **The White Hart** Black Conté chalk, 12" x 16"

ERNEST SAVAGE

with cotton wool (absorbent wool), brushing off as before. Then pastel the whole sky with your lightest cobalt, adding your lightest grey or lightest purple to the horizon. Treat this as a cloudless sky, but try to get gradation of tone from the zenith to the horizon. It will be important to use your pastels very gently on the sky, so that you can work the belt of trees over the top of it. Make sure your trees appear at varying distances away by making the more distant ones cooler and greyer. Treat the bridge as broadly as before, and make something of the reflections of those bright red willows on the far bank. Look for a colour contrast in the old river boats, and make sure their reflections are tonally correct.

The figures are incidental. They happened to be there when I made the sketch, and they were put in quite boldly and almost with one stroke of the chalk. Use light red (26) and reddish grey (28) for the heads of the figures, and be careful you don't make them too large. Try out a few figures on a spare piece of paper. If they 'come off', do the same in your picture. Later in the book there will be a special chapter on the introduction of figures into landscape. While you are painting this picture, you should keep constantly in your mind the direction of light. The sun shines from right to left, lighting up the bridge and front of the inn. The side of the inn, the lean-to and the Brewery board at eave level are in shade. The road over the bridge runs in front of the building and between the two pairs of figures. Wooden plank steps have been set into the river bank to get down to the boats. The river at this point is tidal, and the level of the water is getting towards high tide mark.

Opposite **After the Blizzard**
Cool grey Canson Ingres paper was used to help obtain the wintery effect.

5 Hints on picture making

Importance of pictorial composition

I rate the skill to design pictures successfully as one of the most important of an artist's attributes. A picture will stand or fall on the merit of its design, no matter how well it is painted. Within the limits of this small book, it is only possible to suggest ways to improve your own power of pictorial design. Most amateur painters have a reasonable idea of their ability in this direction. You will know if when on sketching trips you spend hours looking for a suitable subject, or whether you can quickly make up your mind and get down to it. To some extent this is a guide to whether you have a keen perception for a subject or not, for if you take a long time to find something, it could be that you are missing the obvious.

If you think you need to improve your ability to compose pictures, then here are four suggestions which could help you.

(a) Get a good book on this subject alone, and put in some concentrated study.

(b) Take every opportunity to visit art galleries and museums. See how the Masters tackled this problem. Watch your local art shows and begin to make your own assessment of what is good.

(c) Regard all you see in your daily routine as something to compose. Mentally discuss with yourself the problems of arranging this picture you may never paint. At least you are giving thought to composition. If you can, make numerous trial sketches and alternative layouts during odd free moments.

(d) On suitable occasions stop listening to television and *look* instead. Study the pictorial composition of the broadcast picture. These T.V. producers have a flair for pictorial arrangement, and the quality in this department of television is usually top class. When the opportunity occurs, grab your sketch book and draw from the T.V. screen. The very rough drawing with a ball-point pen and the first piece of paper to hand (fig. 47) was just such an occasion, when seconds had to suffice to capture the saddened crowd at Westminster Hall paying their last tribute to Sir Winston Churchill.

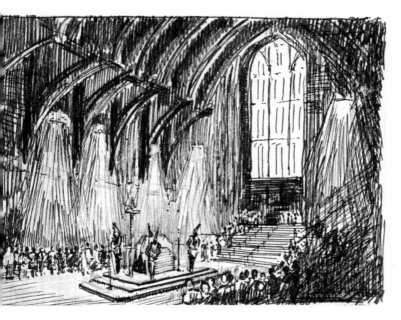

Fig. 47

Hints on composition

It is generally easier for a beginner to be told what to avoid, and to be told in such a way that the idea is understandable and will stick in the memory. Thus I often tell my pupils to avoid 'Union Jack' compositions. In other words:-

Don't let your picture be divided in half either way.

Don't let things of interest run into the corners.

Don't let your lay-out be in equal partitions (fig. 48).

With our two eyes we tend to observe as in an oval. If we shut one eye and look through a telescope we see as a circle. People are going to look at our pictures with two eyes, so arrange it in the natural way, as an oval, and do not draw attention to the corners (fig. 50).

Don't only think of the objects in your picture as outlines. Think of them as areas or shapes. See that you get variety in your shapes, especially those *outside* the objects, like the sky patches between the trunks of trees, the shapes around shadows, or in between buildings (fig. 49).

You must try and make your pictures invite people to look at them, and then look into them, by the way you place your interest or focal point. The onlooker's eye should be led into the picture so that it comes to rest on the interesting part of it. I remember a well known artist once remarking that if the work of some amateurs were placed side by side, the result would be one continuous field. This is because so many choose to draw as if facing squarely the scene before them. The result is a series of lines parallel with the bottom of the picture, which block the way in.

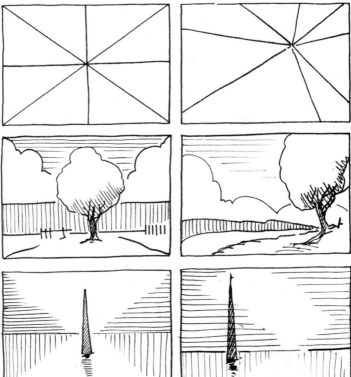

Fig. 48 'Union Jack' designs . . . improved

Selecting subject matter for pastel

Without doubt certain subjects suit the pastel medium. There must have been the occasion when you felt the work on hand might have been more successful had you been painting it in a different medium; for oils, watercolour, gouache etc., like pastel, seem to have a type of subject that suits them best. Subjects with strong contrast of light and shade are often very effective in pastel, and are more readily executed in this medium. Subjects that do well in oils usually go well in pastel, and often the latter is used for studies for pictures finally to be painted in oils. Thus you must cultivate an eye for a suitable pastel picture. Still life, flower studies and portraits usually make excellent subjects for pastel. It is usually a little more difficult to select the right landscape.

When out sketching, I make a practice of drawing several trial compositions of a subject that interests me. These are about 3" long, and are kept very simple with just a little dark tone scrubbed in where required. What seems to be the most satisfactory arrangement is then selected. Do make these tentative drawings roughly in proportion to the shape you intend for your final sketch. Try to select simple subjects. Make a picture of the doorway rather than the house, the house rather than the street, and so on. This is where the skill in selection begins.

The odds are against you finding a ready-made composition. You will have to simplify, make omissions and alterations. You must, however, be truthful in the lighting, and not rob objects of their shadows or their reflections. Pastel does not lend itself to too much detail, so stop counting windows, chimneys, or blades of grass.

Fig. 49

Fig. 50

Fig. 51

I am frequently asked by pupils to help them to select a subject, for some find it difficult to discover one for themselves. They are quick to see the possibilities of a suggestion made to them as a rough drawing, and are quite happy to go on from there. But it is best to select your own material. When in doubt, it is sometimes best not to think in terms of a picture at all, and just make a drawing of something close at hand that interests you, such as a group of weeds, the irregular wooden stumps in an old fence, the knotted bole of a tree. Almost always a picture will suggest itself to you while you are mentally absorbed in the actual study. Then on a fresh piece of paper, with slight rearrangement or different placing to left or right, towards top or bottom, the drawing you have made will provide you with a picture.

You will notice that all these suggested subjects, weeds, fence, tree trunks, are objects near to the eye. They are the kind of subjects that help you to get simple material and are generally more satisfactorily composed. Furthermore, you do not have so many problems with the foreground of the picture in this way. These simple subjects should have

Fig. 52

an interesting play of light and shade to make them attractive and lively when drawn in pastel.

The *viewing frame* can often be of great help to a beginner. This is simply a rectangular hole in a card which, when brought up to the eye, limits the field of vision very much as the viewfinder on a camera. You cannot then see too much at once. As in your trial sketches, your viewing frame should be in the same proportion as the picture you intend to paint. As a boy, I used to cut the three sides of a rectangle for a viewfinder in the cardboard cover of my sketch book, and in the true proportion of it. The rectangle was then pushed open like a little door not much larger than a postage stamp, and closed up again when finished with. I think the merit of this idea was that the viewfinder was never lost.

Hints on drawing your subject

If the ability to compose is one of the most important of an artist's gifts, then draughtsmanship must run design a pretty close second. Only continual practice at drawing from observation can secure improvement.

The beginner must make a practice of being able to recognise his eye level when viewing the scene before him, for this should be correctly placed when making the drawing. This is the start to an understanding of perspective. So when you begin to lay out your subject, make a mark on either side of your paper where you suppose your eye level will come in your picture. This will prevent you finishing with a picture which looks as if you were literally up the pole when you drew it, when in fact you were sitting on a stool by the roadside. Of course you could make a picture of the scene looking downwards, as from a rooftop viewpoint. Your eye level from this high place would still be as described, on the *level* of your eye as you looked out above the scene to the horizon. Since you would be making an unusual viewpoint from above, you would not be able to put these eye level marks on this drawing, for everything depicted would be very much below the level of your eyes.

When by the seaside, the horizon is at the level of your eyes, whether you are sitting on the sand or standing on the cliff top. You can place the horizon in a drawing at any level you choose, depending upon what emphasis you are going for, i.e., a cloud study with low horizon, a landscape

Fig. 53

with hills with high horizon. Remember *you* have chosen where the horizon will be placed, but it will always represent the level of your eye.

When looking at a landscape rolling away from you, the earth and all upon it robs you of a view of the natural horizon, as in a seascape, because many objects between your eyes and the horizon are taller than you are and obstruct the true horizon. It is nevertheless still possible for you to judge where your eye level comes in what you are observing, and to make an indication of it on your drawing.

This eye level is important, because it can be used as a check for your perspective. All horizontal lines that run away from you appear to go *downwards* to this level if they are above the level of your eyes, and to go *upwards* if below this level (figs. 53, 54).

Soft pencil, charcoal, Conté, ink can be used for a drawing afterwards to be used for pastel. Make as good a drawing of your composition as possible, for then when you start to apply the soft pastel you will know approximately where you want it to go.

As you become more practiced at placing your subject on paper, it should be possible to make use of only the arterial lines of a composition, done with charcoal or the pastel itself, and to draw as you use the pastel. This requires judgement and some skill and confidence, which become apparent in the finished work done in the direct manner.

Fig. 54

Fig. 55 **Autumn on the South Downs** Pastel, 19″ x 25″

ERNEST SAVAGE

Selection of paper for special subjects

We have considered the use that can be made of the various surfaces of paper and how we can make the tone of the paper work for us. We should now give thought to the colour of the paper for special purposes.

Most paper manufacturers will send a sample swatch of their products if you write to them. It is very valuable to get one of these, for the whole range of tint and colour can be examined and suitable papers ordered by post. When selecting a paper for an intended picture, keep in mind how the tint of it will assist you or provide the kind of effect you hope to achieve. Warm browns and fawns are useful for autumnal studies (fig. 55), and the cool blue grey papers are more suited for winter. It is sometimes possible to leave a sky untouched, or only brightened a little with pastel at the horizon, if the right shade of pale grey paper is used. Areas of paper not covered with pastel tend to appear to be more luminous, and the most should be made of this tendency. Grey green papers are good for tree subjects, where paper is left for the foliage in shade. Darker blue grey tints in papers can be used to represent any general shadow areas.

Obviously dark subjects need more pastel if painted on light papers, and as we have seen in our first demonstration painting, it is sometimes useful to rub some light tone into the sky when a darker paper is used.

You can prepare your own colour tone using a watercolour or gouache wash on white paper. Indeed it is sometimes most effective if you prepare a background wash of local colours in full variety, pastelling on top when the wash is dry. At all times think of your paper as a *tone,* that is to say, as a degree in the scale from the lightest to darkest part of your picture. You will then find your thoughtful consideration of the tints of papers for various subjects well worth while.

Another exercise from my sketchbook

Enough of theory for a moment; let us do another pastel painting together. Turning over the pages of a recent holiday sketchbook, I found an upright drawing of an interesting corner at San Michele, a suburb of Rapallo, Italy.

Fig. 56 **The Gift Shop, San Michele**

The Gift Shop, San Michele: Stage one

Draw a rectangle 12½″ x 8½″ on a sheet of fawn Ingres paper, and make an outline drawing in charcoal or ink. A Japanese pentel was used for the original sketch. You could draw the composition in pencil, and when correct go over the pencil lines in ink, for we need some of the ink lines to show through the colour work. This gift shop selling toys and postcards for the beach faces the blue Mediterranean Sea. The shadows on the ground in the left-hand corner were made by a large date palm. Under another such palm I placed my sketching stool, and to the delight of the Italian shopkeeper began to draw his display in front of the building, which was built on arches which form the seafront of this little fishing village.

I wanted a simple composition and chose the activity below the archway as the centre of interest. The half-tone reproduction of this picture is of the actual sketch done in colour, and so unfortunately you miss the contrast of the bright blue shop blind and the indian red plaster of the walls. The whole sketch outline and colour was completed on the spot in less than an hour. It is fairly free from fussy detail, and quite obviously was direct in the manner of painting.

Stage two, Fig. 57

The wall area above the main arch as far up as the two advertisements was left almost free of pastel, except where the drainpipe went over it. The darker area at the top half of the same wall received a cross light from the sun which explains the direction of shadow. Start pastelling the darker part of this wall each side of the drainpipe with indian red (16), introducing number 17 of the same colour towards the shuttered window and up to its plaster surround. On the right of this window use indian red (16), adding warm grey (37) for the shadow portion that runs down into the corner behind the blind. Indian red (18) was used for the wall in sunlight above the shop. Use warm grey (37) for the dark under the arch, with cool grey (39) and blue grey (53) for the very dark recesses inside the shop door, inside the open shutter, and underneath the lower verandah on the right. The shadow in the left corner top and bottom and the narrow arch left was put in with warm grey (37), as was the dark side of the drainpipe and the shadows under the postcard stand and on the ground between the various figures.

The iron work of all the verandahs was bright green, and care was taken to use this colour to suggest light and shade, viz., terre vert (62) for darker parts, vivid greens like 63 and 65 for lighter, brighter parts, and some of the ink drawing was allowed to show through. The shuttered windows were done in similar fashion.

Stage three

The final touches were to all the parts that were strongly lit, and the bright accents of colour gave the Mediterranean seaside touch. The left-hand wall was worked with indian red (18) and red orange (11), and the closed windows were suggested with light green (57), for this part was in strong sunlight. For the two Kodak notices above the arch yellow ochre (7) was used, with a touch of a dull red (13) at the top and bottom of them. Cobalt (49) was used for the top of the shop blind, with a line of ultramarine (46) top and bottom for the blue in shade. The wavy tassel edge and indication of lettering on the blind flap was done with white. The goods on the steps were suggested with lighter yellows and dull reds, but one small quarter inch square of intense orange red (9) was put in just where the blind support joined the wall. This gave a contrasting punch to the blue of the blind. Light red (25, 26) was used for the flesh tints of the figures, the deeper for the shaded parts. For the sunlit part of the man's shirt yellow ochre (8) was used, and for the teenager's blouse pale yellow (3) and for her jeans very light blue (50). This last colour was also used in rectangular patches with grey green (71) for the postcards on the stand. Finally the hot sunlit pavement was put in with pale orange (11) and yellow ochre (6).

I wish you could have seen this little sketch in full colour, but if you study the colours I have mentioned and compare them with those in the colour chart in the previous chapter, you should get a fair idea of this typical continental scene.

6 Let's go sketching

It's about time we went out together in our imagination and enjoyed a day's sketching. I can then help you with the kind of problems a beginner has to face outdoors. We covered the equipment needed for such a trip in Chapter Two. This must be collected together for the start.

Protecting pastels: cleaning them

If you are going by car, the weight of your gear is no problem, but sometimes you need to pack a bag and go by bus or train. Then you do need to watch the weight, or you will arrive at the sketching site too exhausted to work. However you travel, you must protect your pastels. See they are well padded with cotton wool (absorbent cotton), for constant shaking about does not improve them. Moreover the smaller pieces tend to get very dirty and difficult to distinguish. It is as well to see your pastels are clean before you take them out. This is a very easy matter. Put all the little bits of pastel a handful at a time into a screw-capped jar, and cover them with ground rice, sawdust, or some other granular substance. A few shakes and turns, so that the rice is well mixed with the pastels, is all that is necessary. Turn out the contents on to a sheet of newspaper, and you will find the pieces gleaming in their true colours, ready to be popped into a cotton wool lined box with compartments for the blues, the greens, the reds etc. By keeping them this way in a box, they do not soil one another so readily, and they are more easily distinguished for tone and tint.

For long distance trips on foot, I sometimes almost fill a large plastic jar with 200 or more bits of pastel, and top it up with ground rice or sawdust. This I slip in my sketching bag knowing I won't have to worry about breakages and that as I move, the pastels are cleaning themselves. This does mean they have to be turned out, and when sketching is over both rice and pastels are poured back into the jar. Paper covered sticks of pastel travel fairly well, and sometimes a selection of the most useful ones are taken as spares. For studio use it is best to have cleaned pastels in partitioned boxes.

Protecting the pastel paintings

It is just as important to consider how you will protect your work so that it is not unduly rubbed on the way home. The drawing board with the fillet surround (wooden frame), also mentioned in Chapter Two, is probably the safest method of carrying pastel drawings, which should be interleaved with thin newspaper or transparent sheet acetate. A good second best is a simple, light-weight plywood board upon which all your sheets of paper and tissues, acetate, and pastel drawings are held together with two large rubber bands. If your board is larger than your sketching bag, it will need to have a string handle to carry it comfortably.

To lessen the number of articles to be carried, I fix my board and paper to my easel which, like the one illustrated earlier, becomes a carrier for board or canvas when folded up. You want to work out the easiest way to pack and carry all that is required, and to devise a scheme for checking that nothing is left behind before you set out for a day's sketching or at your painting location.

The sketching trip

I am always full of expectant leasure when setting out early in the morning on a sketching trip. All my gear has been carefully checked over the night before. I keep a list of essentials so nothing is forgotten. On a fine morning in my suppressed excitement everything I see is a picture, even while waiting for the train or the bus. Weather conditions do not worry me unduly now, in fact I often find an unexpected subject from the shelter of an old shed when it is raining, or I discover an interior to work on.

Today I am taking you to one of my favourite sketching grounds in the heart of Sussex. Not far from Horsham, down a winding lane which runs southwards to Storrington and the South Downs, is a lovely old farm with a medley of barns and buildings and all the paraphanalia of agricultural machinery spread about on both sides of the road. Centuries ago this farmhouse was one of the meeting places of that infamous hanging judge, 'Bloody Jefferies'. Court sessions were held here and his victims summarily dispatched by hanging in an outhouse across the adjoining field. 'Sessions' Farm has no gruesome air about it now. It is delightful in its rural serenity and I have sketched here in every season of the year.

Fig. 59 **Sessions House Farm** Pastel, 19″ x 25″

Working outdoors: selecting the subject

Almost the first thing to do after getting all the gear out of the car is to begin to contemplate the scene, looking for likely compositions. Several of these are illustrated in the next pages, with two of them in colour. At least they will give you a good idea what this farm is like. As we walk up and down the lane, we need to make up our minds as quickly as we can upon our view point, and where we are going to sit in order to be somewhat out of the way. Are we going for a close up, or a more distant view? It's a bright sunny morning, and I am attracted by the stately oak trees that border the lane, the old fence beneath them and the trailer lying on the left-hand verge. From my stool the sitting view is good, and as I begin to erect the easel I survey the scene before me and think what to make of it.

Fig. 60

Fig. 61

The Farm in the Lane: stage one

The brilliant morning light suggests a new approach. Let us work on white cartridge paper (an inexpensive drawing paper) rather than the usual tinted Ingres. A novel start creates more interest, as watercolour washes are mixed up, later to be painted loosely over the smooth side of the paper.

I have already drawn the rough composition of the picture in my sketch book, so that the relative positions of all items in it are now familiar to me. I put my easel slightly lower than usual, until it is almost level. Now the wash will run down slowly. Then without any drawing at all, I put in a light sky of French ultramarine and light red, stopping short at the horizon. Into the sky the darker areas of the nearest tree and the buildings are painted, using yellow ochre and a darker mixture of the first named colours. Pure yellow ochre, diluted with water, is allowed to pick up the initial wash at the horizon and is brought down to the bottom of the paper, catching up the darker areas in so doing The paper is now completely covered. While very wet, a mixture of Permanent Yellow and a little blue helps to create the brighter green in the immediate foreground. It looks nothing at all like the scene, for all the colours have run into one another, giving a rather soft, loose effect upon which we will draw and pastel when dry. You may think there is something very chancy about washing in local colour without any lines of composition. It is not as fortuitous as you think, for after all most of this wash is going to be overpainted with opaque pastel. Of course there is nothing to stop you putting in a pencil outline if you wish.

Stage two, Fig. 60

The wash is quite dry, so the composition is briefly indicated with a light grey pastel, for black pastel or charcoal would tend to destroy the light I am trying to retain. I begin to pastel the sky and distance, making quite sure there is gradation of tone in the sky. The work is started on the middle distance trees, which need to be greyer than those near at hand. I then make a feature of the shadow portions of the foreground oak tree, carefully depicting its branch formation, and follow this with the warm darks of the barn and its even darker interior. The wash for the left-hand trees had faded away, and this suggests the idea of keeping the space between the trees on either side of the road wider than it actually is, to help the arrangement.

The remaining details are then put in, with some thought for the roofs of the buildings, allowing a bluish touch where the slates are facing a blue sky and a warmer colour for the red tiles that are catching the sunlight. All the time during the painting the bright light is uppermost in my mind. It is this I want to capture.

After Haymaking: Fig. 61

This is an early evening painting of the same farm in midsummer. I have gone a little closer to the buildings to make the painting. You will see that the shadows are longer, and there is that pinky glow in the sky that gives sure indication of the time of day. Notice the difference the paper makes in these two drawings. The rougher texture of the white paper gives a brighter and more startling effect. In the second, a pale grey Canson Ingres was used, and this tends to make a more harmonious and quieter picture.

This was a very quick sketch, to capture the evening light. The design was drawn with charcoal, and then the sky was boldly and directly painted with two tones of red grey pastel (the lighter for the horizon), again remembering this all important gradation. The effect of this sky painting was to set up the dark tree masses and other areas in shade so, continuing to paint the light, bright neutral yellows were used for the surface of the sunlit lane. The buildings were painted with direct strokes that either ran with the perspective of them, or roughly indicated the texture of boards and tiles. The colourful accents of the tractor and the groups of farm workers who had just returned from haymaking were the final touches to this study, which in all took about an hour to do.

In describing the work on the two colour reproductions, this time I have avoided numbering the pastel colours used to do them. It will make a good exercise for you now to select your own.

Some problems when sketching outdoors

It is grand to go out sketching, and this really is the only way to keep your work and yourself fresh. You must expect to encounter difficulties. Try to overcome them without getting into a flap, and without becoming despondent about your work. You must learn to face the uncertainties of weather and to adjust yourself to all conditions so that your work will go on. You must be quick to extemporise when, for instance, the wind begins to rock your easel, for you must find some means to anchor it. You will combat the flies and gnats, and endure unpleasant smells if you are really keen. The less fussy you become about these things, the less you will be put off and the more your work will improve.

The only way to capture the wondrous beauties of nature is to go out for them. It cannot be done at home. The sketching gear is always a problem, and with pastel drawings to carry a little special care is needed, though certainly no more than you would expect to give to a wet oil. So learn to protect your pastel pictures with sheets of cover paper, the smoother the better. When you have worked with pastels for some time, you will be surprised at the wear and tear they will take. After all, pastels are comparatively easy to touch up again (by sweeping off) if some part of the work has been accidentally smeared.

Fig. 62

This rough drawing of
Sessions Farm is the kind of
composition one makes in a
sketch book. Several alternative
arrangements may be made
before you are satisfied. I made
a 19″ x 25″ pastel of this
design, which is shown in
fig. 59.

Fig. 63

Fig. 64 **Factory Smoke** Black chalk

The city and industrial subjects

Most of us are unfortunately chained by our employment to
the large cities. As sketchers we can make use of this by
getting variety into our work and not losing the opportunity
of capturing the industrial scene. There are subjects
galore in large towns. One of my sketching haunts is the
Pool of London. For me, the constant activity on London's
river and around dockland is of tremendous interest. So let's
go off together once again and mingle with the very early
morning workers at Monument Station as we carry our gear
past this historic column, by the bustle of the fish market at
Billingsgate and down to the Thames. We are going to make
a drawing of Tower Bridge, and having found a spot to
dump the gear we are eager to find our subject. Yes, there

it is; characteristic in the misty morning, Tower Bridge dominates the river at this point. From where we stand we see the toy-like red grey buses crawl their way over it. Behind is the pearly pink flush of the morning sky, pushing its way into the city smoke. Nearby derricks sway and dip, feeding the cargo boats with crates and bales. Patches of smoke wisp up from little tugs, obscuring the bulky barges and blotting out for a moment the distant work on the wharf.

'What are we going to make of all this, as a picture', we mutter, and as if answering a thousand questions we reiterate 'keep it simple', 'keep it simple'! And so we begin the tentative sketches. Tower Bridge is pushed back to be less important in our picture. We give more stress to the Customs House and Pier, and part of it is made to cover some of the bridge so that its mast cuts the upper gallery of the bridge. Barges are drawn in and placed so as to balance the darker mass of the Customs Pier, which now holds an important place on its green stained piles. We lose and find the familiar shape of Tower Bridge with passing smoke and haze, and then re-check the main ingredients of our picture. At last we are satisfied. The anxious moment is over, for now our drawing is ready for pastelling to begin.

Early morning in the port of London

Now you have a go. Make a good drawing from the double page half-tone picture (fig. 65), on a medium grey Ingres paper. Not less than a size of 12″ x 16″, but preferably 15″ x 20″. When you are satisfied with your drawing, begin to paint the sky with your pastels. To help you I have made a list of the pastels used for this picture in the approximate order that you will apply them.

Use these pastels

Sky From zenith to horizon Cool grey (39, 40, 41), red grey (29), light red (27), cool grey (41).
Tower Bridge Leave paper, but touch up with cool grey (39).
River At horizon cool grey (41), then pale olive green (59) with wavelets in foreground Indian red (18) and various greys.
Customs pier and barges Cool grey (39), raw umber (34), grey green (69). Various greys to tone.

Fig. 65 **Early Morning in the Pool of London** Pastel, 16″ x 20″

7 Recreative and holiday painting

Leisure painting

More and more people are taking up sketching and painting in what leisure time can be squeezed into the daily routine, because of the change it gives and the relaxation it provides for the mind. Many turn to painting possibly because it interested them in their schooldays. Some want a new challenge, the 'I can't draw a straight line, can I be taught to paint' types. The young who turn to painting and other forms of art, do so, in the main, with a career in mind.

No matter what the incentive, almost everyone who takes up this kind of hobby finds it absorbing and full of pleasure. As interest increases, there follows the desire to improve, and books like this are designed to help you with your early difficulties and to save your time, since the authors share with you the experience of a lifetime.

Some people who want to start to sketch late in life are sometimes diffident about joining a class in a local Art School, or College for Adult Education. Be assured, there are many like you, and one of the first things you should do if you get keen about painting is to make enquiries of the facilities offered by your local Educational Authority in Great Britain, or by the adult education division of your local school system in the United States. You will be surprised at the opportunity that exists.

Art clubs and societies

The more ambitious, and perhaps socially minded, tend to join the local art clubs that are spread all over the country. This is a fine idea, for you meet people with common interests and, as your work improves, you are able to take part in their exhibitions. Some of the larger societies run special weekend courses, and on these occasions professional painters are engaged to give lecture demonstrations, painting instruction to club members, and criticism of their work.

Art books and magazines

Some amateur painters prefer to plough a lone furrow, and keep up to date with their work by reading a regular art

Fig. 66 **Yachts at Rapallo** Pastel, 15″ x 22″

magazine, or the many books on painting that now adorn the
shelves of libraries and book shops. Sooner or later, the
weekend painter will want to go on an extended excursion,
for a short intensive course of study with a practicing artist,
or else alone, or with a sketching group for a holiday at
home or abroad. I have just returned from such a trip to
Italy.

Painting holidays abroad

It is a wonderful experience to go to a foreign country to
paint, for the strange and unusual scenes can be very stimulating. There are a number of organisations that run continental painting holidays, so it is not difficult to join up with
a group going abroad. Some prefer to do it alone, or with
another painting companion. Whichever way you choose, the
excitement that accompanies foreign travel is intensified if
you have a purpose, especially if the purpose is to paint.

Gear for long distance travel

Unless you are touring by car, special attention has to be paid to the painting equipment to be taken. You must study the weight, and there will come the time when you have to decide whether you will take that other garment, or the extra box of pastels. The problem is increased when you want to work in several media, for oils, watercolours and pastels can all feel like a ton when you are carrying them yourself. The best solution for a keen pastellist is to take a box or a plastic jar of pieces, packed out with wool, absorbent cotton, sawdust, or ground rice. My own, described earlier, weighs under two pounds when filled. This selection of pastel pieces can be supported with a set of pastel pencils, called Othello, and your normal sketching pencils and pens. You need to take only a minimum of paper in case you are in some out of the way place for a time, for on the continent you can purchase papers as you want them, and have fun doing so. This can be funnier than you think, if you cannot speak the language. On a recent trip I discovered my lightweight sketching stool had been left behind. Another had to be bought in a large Italian city. So that I could work, the task of buying the stool was given to my wife and her friends. They spent the whole day squatting in various shops in order to describe by actions what was wanted. They didn't succeed in getting it, but were offered all kinds of intriguing things.

Fig. 67

Getting the atmosphere

Painting in foreign parts is something of an adventure. There is so much to see and do. The more we record our impressions with little line drawings, the better we shall be able to appreciate the atmosphere of the place and portray it.

Gondolas at rest

I envy all who have yet to see Venice for the first time. It is a most inspiring experience. I never tire of painting the Venetian scene. This is a wonderful city, that seems to compel you to work harder to capture its many beauties. The line drawing in fig. 68 was done with a felt-tripped pen, and was intended for a picture in pastel. The two gondolas moored before a typical Venetian arched doorway made a fairly simple composition. The next day passing the same spot aboard a gondola, I noticed two gondoliers were stretched out fast asleep in the afternoon heat on these very boats. This human interest made the picture, but alas it is one of many still to be done. Time is an important consideration when on a foreign holiday, and I believe it is better to record numerous impressions and to bring back one or two fewer finished pictures.

Fig. 68

'Early Morning, Venice'

It is my experience that you get the true feel of a place in the early morning. It is certainly the best time for pastelling in busy places like Venice. At this time such interesting colour effects can be seen, and you are fresh to enjoy them.

My picture 'Early Morning, Venice' (fig. 69) began as a study of one gondola, having discovered how difficult they were to draw. Then the vertical group of piles and posts around the boat were seen to look well before the single toned mass of San Georgio across the lagoon, with the morning light streaming in to provide the extra glint on the almost still surface of the water.

Light being the important effect, watercolour was used as a backing to this picture as a general wash of local colour previously described, but with the difference that the toned mass of San Georgio was an important shape, and had to be accurately drawn. This silhouette was left in the watercolour medium, and all before it was painted in with pastel.

Fig. 69 **Early Morning, Venice** Pastel. 11" x 15"

Using pastel pencils

These are very useful lightweight adjuncts to the soft pastel when travelling long distances. The Carb-Othello pastel pencils are made by the Swan Pencil Co. They are made in sixty colours, are easy to sharpen, and very pleasant to use. They are sold in boxed sets from 12 upwards, and are made as pencils in wood and as square sectioned sticks like normal hard chalks. I have a box of 24 pencils and 24 chalks mostly in the neutral tints of the greys and browns. With these I can start off an important drawing and leave it when pressed for time to be completed with soft pastel on my return. The makers are very helpful, and if you write for information they will gladly supply it.

Portofino re-visited

I have spent many happy days painting in Portofino. Here you can sit at any of the numerous harbourside cafes and make your pictorial impressions of this delightful fishing village, and at the same time revel in the warm Italian sunshine. Only a few weeks ago I took a group of pupils here for a day's sketching. We arrived quite early in the morning by bus from Rapallo, and immediately I set up the easel and spread out the gear among the cluster of boats on the slipway. This faces the natural harbour, which is an inlet between two mountainous ridges. All round are the tall colourful buildings that rear themselves up on both sides as if challenging the rocky slopes into which they have been built. The houses are many storied of various heights and widths, with many supported on arches or having a shop or cafe at ground level. Portofino is always full of life and interest, and the great temptation is to try and depict too much of it at once.

I had to give a demonstration on the spot, so I went for a close-up of the lower parts of the buildings, the arches and shop blinds, the gaily coloured continental sun shades covering the stalls of the work of the lace makers, and I included some boats and their reflections.

A Portofino demonstration, Fig. 70

I selected a whole sheet of warm grey Fabriano Ingres and made my first layout drawing with an Othello pastel pencil, warm medium grey, which was somewhat darker than the paper. Architectural subjects of this kind need careful drawing, particularly the arches and the detail of the various shuttered windows. It is important on occasions to get away from your work, for you come back with a freshened eye. Often before you have sat down, you can observe a number of corrections you want to make.

I got to work on this picture right away by indicating with firm direct strokes the tall corner buttress, left centre of the picture. Three or four light toned pastels were used for this, ending in the warm grey cement rendering at the base. It was important that the face of this wall appeared to stand out in front of the wall of the houses to the right. The local colour was kept lower in tone for this right-hand wall, and the plaster tints quickly suggested with broad downward strokes, leaving the grey paper where shadows occurred under blinds and arches. I then loosely and boldly pastelled the interest around the sunshades and the display of goods before the darkened arches, and the deep darks in the vicinity of the blinds and the arch. Thus in a few minutes the highest and lowest tones were established, and the picture was gradually brought on as a whole after that. The demonstration lasted about two hours, for all processes were described at the time of their taking place.

Midday at Portofino, Fig. 71

The second colour plate was not done as a demonstration, so I was able to proceed more leisurely with it, and about two hours were spent drawing it with the Othello pencils in several tints. This second viewpoint looked back on the spot where the first picture was painted.

I used a warm gingery brown Canson Ingres for this painting, the true colour of which you will see in the unpainted parts of the water at the bottom left-hand corner. I set out to try and capture the heat of Portofino during the middle of the day, and to register the bright noon light that glared up from the cobbles and the roof tops.

Once the light effect had been obtained and a note taken of the local colour, no more work was done on this picture until it was taken home. Herein lies the advantage of the pastel pencil, for you are able to record a great deal of information about your subject as the drawing proceeds in colour. The work does not need any special protection either, and soft pastel can be applied over the pastel pencil drawing in the serenity of the studio.

Fig. 70

Fig. 71

SANTA FRUTTUOSO

ERNEST SAVAGE

Fig. 72

8 Figures in landscape

I remember seeing a film some time ago about a secret weapon that had been used against the civilians in a country village. Because of it all life had disappeared, and as the cameras panned round the square, although a door was open here and there and a curtain moved in the wind, not a living thing could be seen among the old half-timbered Tudor buildings. It was a grim picture, and it sent a chill down the spine.

I get this kind of feeling when I see pictures representing villages and farms in which the painter has dodged putting in the passing figure or the odd hen. You must try and put life into your landscapes, for you are rarely completely alone when you paint your pictures. I agree there are some views that need solitude, and you should decide while you are sketching if you do not wish to share the scene with anybody else.

Improving your skill with figures

You don't need a long training in life drawing to be able to put a figure in your landscapes. The study of the proportion of the human body helps you considerably, but it is far more important to observe how it moves. The habit of making numerous quick sketches of people anywhere you happen to be is invaluable, however rough the sketches are. Begin by drawing a part of the building before you, say a shop entrance, then start to watch the people going in and out. Be content first to place the head at the correct height, i.e., in relation to the door or window. Then get head and feet correctly placed, not worrying too much about what goes on between them. In this way you build up a store of information all based upon your own observation. Remember you only need one person to be able to draw a crowd, if you continually draw him as he moves about. In my pastel (fig. 73) of the children leaving their school to go to church, I used two girls. I got them to walk from the doorway across the courtyard, over the lawn, backwards and forwards for about twenty minutes, and as you see, by that time I had put in thirty or forty boys and girls directly with pastel. At the time, the two girls thought I was quite mad, until they saw the result of their meanderings, and how I had fixed where their heads and feet appeared in relation to the whole scene.

Fig. 73

How and where to place figures

Although you must aim at putting your figures in natural places, some thought has to be given to the balance of the composition and how the figures will help it. Figure interest should be within the oval of vision, and not be allowed to slip into the corners. Think of your figures as groups of two's and threes, sometimes covering parts of one another up, rather than as isolated single persons. Let your figures be matey. Join the figures in a group together, with shadow, or an extended arm, and place them to support your centre of interest (figs. 74, 75).

If you are in doubt regarding position, you can always cut out a paper figure of the right size, and move it about your drawing until you are satisfied. Remember the correct placing of figures depends upon *your* viewpoint or eye level when painting the picture. If you leave out the pygmies, there is very little difference in the height of adults. Therefore, if you are standing up to paint and the ground before you is level, then the heads of all the people standing before you are approximately level with your own.

Fig. 74 Figures above eye level

Fig. 75 **The Salmon Pool** Pastel, 19" x 25"

Figures with pastel

Small incidental figures can only be suggested with pastel, detailed features are impossible. You go for the inclination of the head in one red brown blob. Then give an indication by the cast shadow where the feet start. As a general rule the shadow on the body links up and becomes part of the cast shadow. As for the body itself, this is almost always expressed by drawing the parts that catch the light.

It is often a good idea to place figures in light against dark backgrounds. Figures in shade appear as almost silhouettes. Don't be afraid to include figures in your pictures. Make lots of practice shots on another piece of paper, until you are fairly confident. After all, if you place them badly, it is so easy to sweep them off with a brush and have another go.

9 Using photographs

I am so often asked if it is all right to use photographic material for making pictures, that some brief reference must be made to this subject. Years ago, it was certainly not the thing to make use of photographs for painting important pictures. Artists were supposed to get on with the job without mechanical aids. Even now, there is a kind of slur attached to the phrase, 'he paints from photographs', as though referring to some delinquent engraver making some spare cash in the cellar.

There is no doubt that as far as a commercial artist is concerned, he must have access to a vast supply of photographic material, depending upon the type of work he does. For him it is an essential time and money saver. The portrait painter can dispense with some of the sittings if he has pictorial reference of the model, or even the costume being worn at the time. These examples can be extended, but one thing is certain, if you ask the professional which he would prefer to be using, he will most certainly ask for the real thing, and rate the photograph as second best.

In our struggles as amateurs to paint pictures, if a photograph will help, I see no reason why it should not be used. In a sense we are painting for the fun of it, so surely we can do as we wish. When it comes to landscape painting, even in the day of the colour transparency, you rarely see a satisfactory composition from the painting point of view, and to become too dependent upon this sort of mechanical process is most surely going to end in your work becoming dull and lifeless. So keep your photographs for the incidental reference of detail.

Nothing can compete with painting direct from nature and those occasions when with zest and enthusiasm you cannot wait to get started. It is this that gives vitality to your work, and for this reason I have so often repeated the advice about the habit of constant sketching and designing.

It is idle to deny that the camera has its uses, particularly in a moment of action or movement. It would be most useful to have, for instance, a collection of cloud studies, especially in colour. A good deal could be learned from this, though I have no experience of such a thing myself. The movement of figures and animals could also be studied in this way, and might produce greater dexterity when you attempt to draw these from life, as you must do if you want to achieve a 'lively' quality in your work.

By all means use a camera for photographing your own work. This is a good way to keep a record of what you have done, especially if you sell or give your work away from time to time. A black and white photograph of a painting will most certainly reveal if your tones are reasonably correct, and this is a great help.

Fig. 76 **Sunshine Before the Storm, Rapallo** Pastel, 15″ x 22″, on fawn Fabriano Ingres paper. The camera reveals the true strength of the tone depicted in the storm clouds.

10 Pastel with other media

It is quite a common practice for oil painters to use pastels and chalks for making studies. This has been so for hundreds of years. It is not so usual for pastels to be used in conjunction with water bound paints. It interested me a great deal to learn the other day that the large priceless cartoons by Raphael in the Queen's Collection were being restored at the Victoria and Albert Museum by artist craftsmen using pastels. This surely says something for the reliability of the soft pastel.

Pastels and watercolour

Mention has already been made of the effective use of watercolour washes as backings for pastel work. Pastels can also be used on a finished watercolour or one that has been taken further than the initial wash. Beginners will find it is quite interesting to work with pastel on one of their watercolour failures. So long as the subject and the design is right, there is no reason at all why a successful pastel could not be made this way. I remember once painting a watercolour of the fish market in Venice. Towards the end, I had an unfortunate accident with it and it became badly splashed with water. It was put into the portfolio with disgust and disappointment, but on discovering it a year or so later, I saw what a fine pastel subject it would have made. I began working on the watercolour with pastel, at first as a trial, then got interested and finally finished it. This picture was the first to sell in a London exhibition a few weeks later.

Pastels for interior subjects

It is quite a fascinating task to paint an interesting interior. I get carried away by those full of junk, and make it a point to remember where such subjects have been discovered, so they can be tackled when it is better to work under cover. Small pictures of subjects full of detail are really not for the pastellist, so if you like this kind of pictorial material you should work as large as you can.

When you are confronted with a mass of objects in a barn or shed, it is still important to simplify and to depend upon

Fig. 77 **Interior of a Devon Barn** Pastel, 15″ x 22″

the play of light and shade for the effect you are seeking. Before you start, study your subject with your eyes half closed. My picture of the interior of a dilapidated barn in Devon is typical of this kind of subject. I found the light trickling down over the bales of straw very intriguing, and went for this from an unusual viewpoint, up among the old beams in the roof. It was a most uncomfortable position. The cobwebs hanging from the ancient roof timbers did not help at all and all around was as dry as a tinder box, so I was too scared to smoke.

I decided to settle down to make a good line drawing of the subject, and used sanguine chalk and good stout white paper for the study. The drawing position was so difficult that this was as much as could be attempted, and from the study a full pastel painting could be made. But it did not turn out quite like this. The chalk drawing was done, and without waste of time I climbed back to the ground again. No sooner down, the sun came out, and the effect inside the barn was simply wonderful. There and then I changed my plans, set up the easel in the doorway and began to paint the chalk drawing with watercolours. This didn't go at all well, for the red chalk ran into the colours and deadened the very effect of light that was required. I put the drawing in the sun to dry, hoping my luck would change. It didn't. I was spotted by a painting companion who suggested my car was not very well parked in this old farmyard, and in manoevering around I had the misfortune to run over an old brown duck. This disturbed me considerably, for I then had to go and wring its neck to put it out of its misery. I had never experienced this before in my life. So with the duck hanging forlornly from my hand, I went to find its owner, who surprisingly suggested that we should have it for supper. We did, and it was jolly good.

It was some few days after this incident that I returned to the painting, and finished it with pastel. All the lovely warmth of colour is lost in the reproduction, but you can see how I selected the important parts of the junk - the mangle, the rake, the bags and sacks of goodness knows what, and the litter of planks that lie awkardly over the old horse stalls - and how the shadows have been used to join this conglomeration into some sort of unity.

Pastel and gouache

These make excellent companions because the visual effect
they give is very similar in its opacity. It is quite fascinating
to begin a study in gouache and finish it in pastel. Sometimes it is difficult to tell where the gouache ends and the
pastel begins.

Ink line and pastel

This is another attractive way of working with pastel, and is
a method worthy of considerable experiment. A complete
black and white drawing is made with indian ink and brush.
The picture should be as tonally correct as possible by the
exploitation of ink lines of various thicknesses to show form
and texture. A bold approach is needed with the ink work,
and pastelling starts as soon as the full drawing is made.
The pastel is applied freely, sometimes covering the ink,
sometimes permitting the ink to show through. The result is
usually very effective in its strength and boldness. The
example in this method (fig. 79) is a corner in the ancient
fishing village of Camogli.

Fig. 78

Fig. 79 **In Old Camogli** Ink line and pastel, 15″ x 10″

11 Storing, mounting, framing, fixing

Storing pastel pictures

By far the safest way to keep a pastel painting is to frame it properly. Obviously we cannot frame all our works, studies and unfinished pictures, so care must be taken to store these in such a way that the risk of the surface of them being rubbed is minimised. It is a good thing when a picture is completed to give it a sharp tap on the floor before it is taken off the drawing board, so that the loose chalk particles fall off. Just as we protect for carrying, it is best to store a pastel picture with a sheet of smooth paper fixed to the front of it, before placing it in a tray, drawer, or portfolio. With reasonable care, I have found those kept in portfolios suffer little damage if each is covered with tissue or grease-proof (waxed) paper. It is a little awkward when you want to show your drawings, and for this reason I find ordinary pins are the best to use to seal a picture temporarily. They can so easily be unpinned, and then pinned up again.

Framing and mounting

This is always a rather personal matter, but there is no doubt that the choice of frame can make or mar a picture. The traditional way of framing a pastel is to do so by using a narrow frame and a wide wash lined mount (mat). If a mount about $\frac{1}{4}''$ thick is used, there is no chance of the pastel touching the glass. The continentals frequently frame a pastel actually touching the glass. Sometimes they have a second glass sheet in front of this which passes over the slip and into the main frame. There always seems to me to be a lot of risk attached to this method of framing, and it should be left to those who are expert at it.

Sometimes a pastel looks well close framed like an oil, without a cut mount (mat) but with a wider frame. If a pastel picture is to be framed in this way, it is necessary for a spacing fillet (wooden strip) to be inserted in the rebate (rabbet) between picture and glass, so that the picture is kept away from the glass. This is easily done using $\frac{1}{4}''$ balsa wood, glued above the glass before the picture is put in the frame.

When pastels are painted on heavy papers it is sometimes unnecessary to mount them down (i.e. paste them) on a sheet of white cardboard, for they can be fixed to a cut mount with scotch tape. If a pastel picture is to be close framed, or has been worked on thin Ingres paper, it is best pasted on to a sheet of white cardboard of good quality, not strawboard.

It is quite a tricky business to mount down a pastel. The real secret is to make sure the pastel picture has been dampened with clean water on the back of it, and given time to stretch out. A picture framer will do this work with a batch of pastels, damping them all and setting them aside one on top of the other, interleaved with a very smooth paper. The cardboard then receives its coating of cold water paste, smoothed off with the edge of a piece of waste cardboard. The drawing is lowered gently on to this, with its protecting sheet of smooth paper. The whole is gently rubbed from the centre to remove all air bubbles. It is then allowed to dry under light pressure.

A picture framer will always help you on these matters, although it does save money if you can do some of these things for yourself.

Fixing pastels

On the whole, I prefer not to fix my pastels, but to paste them down on good white cardboard. In this way, some of the paste goes through the paper and helps to stick the back of the chalk particles to it. Largely my opposition to fixing is just prejudice, for some of the new aerosol fixatives are a vast improvement on the old stuff we used to blow on our work years ago. I have tested this new fixative on white paper, and it leaves no stain whatever. Speaking of sprays, I was most amused the other day to be asked quite seriously by one of my woman pupils if I fixed my pastel pictures with hair setting lotion!

Conclusion

We have come a long way together since we set out with our basic materials to make a start with pastel painting. If your interest in this delightful means of self expression has been aroused, and you are keen to pass on from the beginner's stage, this book must have been worthwhile. We all have much to learn, and if you wish to continue, read the recommended books which will take you further along the road, and work hard yourself. Here's wishing you many happy hours with your pastels.

12 Useful information

Pastel exhibitions

In Great Britain the Pastel Society holds annual exhibitions that are open to non-members. All details can be obtained from the Secretary, Royal Institute Galleries, 195 Piccadilly, London, W.1.

In the United States, pastels are shown in the annual exhibitions of the American Watercolour Society in New York and the Philadelphia Watercolour Club.

Books

The Artist's Guide. Artist Publishing Co., London.

The Technique of Pastel Painting by Leonard Richmond. Pitman, London.

Drawing and Painting in Pastel by Jack Merriott. A. & C. Black, London, and Van Nostrand, Princeton, New Jersey and New York.

Pastel Painting: Modern Techniques by Stephen Csoka. Reinhold, New York.

Magazines

The Artist. Artist Publishing Co., London.

American Artist. Watson Guptill Publications.

These are excellent magazines. If you read one that has been produced across the Atlantic, you will find the difference in outlook very stimulating.

Pastel manufacturers etc.

America

M. Grumbacher, Inc., 460 W.34 Street, New York.

F. Weber Co., 1220 Buttonwood Street, Philadelphia 19123, Pa.

Britain

George Rowney & Co., Ltd., 10 Percy Street, London, W.1.

Reeves & Sons Ltd., 178 Kensington High Street, London, W.8.

Winsor & Newton Ltd., 51 Rathbone Place, London, W.1.

France

Lefranc, 15 Rue de la Ville L'Eveque, Paris, 8.

Germany

Swan Pencil Co., Nuremberg.

Holland

Talens and Zoon, Apeldoorn.

Fig. 80. **Arundel Castle** from the Black Rabbit chalk pit

Index